SOMETHING BAD HAPPENED

*By the same author*

**Outsmarting Worry**
An Older Kid's Guide to Managing Anxiety
*Dawn Huebner PhD*
*Illustrated by Kara McHale*
ISBN 978 1 78592 782 9
eISBN 978 1 78450 702 2


*of related interest*

**Alex and the Scary Things**
A Story to Help Children Who Have Experienced Something Scary
*Melissa Moses*
*Illustrated by Alison MacEachern*
ISBN 978 1 84905 793 6
eISBN 978 1 78450 066 5

**I Have a Question about Death**
Clear Answers for All Kids, including Children with Autism
Spectrum Disorder or other Special Needs
*Arlen Grad Gaines and Meredith Englander Polsky*
ISBN 978 1 78592 750 8
eISBN 978 1 78450 545 5

**Can I tell you about Anxiety?**
A guide for friends, family and professionals
*Lucy Willetts and Polly Waite*
*Illustrated by Kaiyee Tay*
ISBN 978 1 84905 527 7
eISBN 978 0 85700 967 8

**Frankie's Foibles**
A story about a boy who worries
*Kath Grimshaw*
ISBN 978 1 84905 695 3
eISBN 978 1 78450 210 2

# SOMETHING BAD HAPPENED

## A KID'S GUIDE TO COPING WITH EVENTS IN THE NEWS

**Dawn Huebner**

*Illustrated by Kara McHale*

Jessica Kingsley *Publishers*
London and Philadelphia

First published in 2019
by Jessica Kingsley Publishers
73 Collier Street
London N1 9BE, UK
and
400 Market Street, Suite 400
Philadelphia, PA 19106, USA

*www.jkp.com*

**Library of Congress Cataloging in Publication Data**
A CIP catalog record for this book is available from the Library of Congress

**British Library Cataloguing in Publication Data**
A CIP catalogue record for this book is available from the British Library

ISBN 978 1 78775 074 6
eISBN 978 1 78775 075 3

# Contents

# Introduction for Parents and Caregivers

You want your children to feel safe. You work hard to keep the steady drip-drip-drip of bad news from them, and to protect them from explosions of bigger news. But children have a way of picking up on things. And sometimes news has implications important enough that we feel compelled to tell our children directly. But how?

When our children inadvertently hear about large-scale tragedies, or when we decide to tell them, what should we say? How do we help them make sense of what they are hearing, and put their fears into perspective? How can we preserve their feelings of safety, and optimism, and strength in the face of scary news?

*Something Bad Happened* was designed to help parents talk to their 6–12-year-olds about serious world events—national and international news of all kinds—although the events are never named. This was done intentionally, for two reasons. First, not naming specific events protects children from casually learning about the wide range of tragedies in our world. You (as parent or caregiver) retain complete control over which events to talk to your children about, and how much information to provide. Second, referring to an unspecified "bad thing" keeps the book flexible so you can use it to talk about a natural disaster for example, and then, sometime later, a human tragedy.

You can use this book to talk about anything that has happened in the world, any kind of bad news, with one significant caveat. Whatever happened cannot have happened to your child. There is an important distinction between hearing about something and experiencing it. This book addresses the former. If your child has experienced something tragic, please seek help from a book about trauma or from a mental health professional.

*Something Bad Happened* is meant to be read by a child (or children) and parent together, or by a child with a parent nearby. The book steps you through a discussion of what happened, where it happened, and why. It addresses common questions and provides tools to calm fears. Pause to allow your children to do the drawing and writing prompts strategically placed to help them process feelings and integrate what they are learning.

Please do not read this book at bedtime. While reassuring in tone, the subject matter is difficult. Most children will need extra cuddles or fun activities to help them shift their attention to other things.

The following 7 pointers are guidelines for parents

talking to children about difficult things. They are included here to help you know when and how to talk about whatever piece of news prompted you to pick up this book:

1. **Monitor your own reaction.** When hearing difficult news, children look to adults for cues about what to think and how to feel. It's okay to let your children know that you are upset but keep in mind that extreme displays of emotion are frightening to children. Try to process your more complicated feelings elsewhere. Maintain a calm presence in front of your children and they will be calmer, too.

2. **Ask your children what they already know,** and what they are thinking and feeling. The answers may surprise you. Children often hear bits and pieces of the news, and then jump to conclusions that leave them needlessly afraid. They personalize what they hear (we all do) and worry from a perspective that is unique to them. Reassure your children while responding calmly and rationally to their questions.

3. **Use simple terms** (especially for younger children) **and skip the gory details** (for all children). Carefully monitor your children's exposure to sensationalized reports and reactions, whether from the media or from the people around them.

4. **Remember that even bright children are still just children.** Children are not little adults. They are more concrete and literal in their thinking. Your words form the basis for their beliefs. Be careful about negative

thinking, sweeping generalizations, and explanations that cast groups of people as bad.

5. **Maintain routines.** Routines are hugely comforting. They help children know what to expect, and signal that all is well. When something bad happens, pay extra attention to maintaining consistency around going to school, eating meals, and going to bed.

6. **Focus on the positive.** Talk about who is helping the victims of a disaster, and what they are doing. Involve your children in a discussion about how your family can contribute. Positive action eases feelings of helplessness and fear.

7. **Watch for changes.** Signs that children are struggling emotionally include problems with sleep, physical complaints, developmental backsliding (becoming more clingy, more needy, less capable), irritability, sadness, and fear. If you notice these signs, provide additional comfort and support. If changes last more than a week, talk to your pediatrician or seek help from a mental health professional.

Resilience is defined as the capacity to recover from adversity. It is an important predictor of health and well-being. By exposing your children to measured bits of real-world events and helping them process their thoughts and feelings, you are helping to build this crucial skill. Together you can learn about, put into perspective, and formulate plans regarding the big bad things happening in our world. Together you can consciously decide to face adversity with optimism and love.

CHAPTER 1

# Something Happened

**Something bad happened.**

It didn't happen to you. It didn't happen on your street. But still, it happened somewhere in the world, and it's affecting lots of people.

You may have noticed the grown-ups around you talking in serious ways. Or making a point of not talking when you are in the room.

You may have noticed that the news is on all the time. Or weirdly, not on at all.

You may have noticed that people around you seem distracted, nervous, angry, sad.

You may be wondering, "What is going on?"

Or maybe you know what's going on, and it's making you feel nervous, or angry, or sad.

When we learn about something bad—even when we hear only bits and pieces of it—our brains get busy trying to make sense of what we've heard. We want to know:

What happened?

Why did it happen?

Will it happen again?

Will it happen to ME?

Talking about what happened is one of the best ways to settle down our brains. Talking helps us understand what happened, and how it might affect us. It helps us figure out what, if anything, we need to do.

But talking can be hard. Especially when it's about something bad. Something scary. Something on everyone's mind.

This book can help.

It will pose questions you and your parents can discuss so you know what happened, and where. It will explain why things like that happen, how common or uncommon they are, and who is working right now to keep you safe.

This book will also help you understand your feelings about whatever happened, and give you tools to help you feel better.

You get to decide how to use this book.

You can read it all at once, or in small pieces.

You can read it with a grown-up who cares about you, or on your own with a grown-up nearby.

You can spend time writing and drawing when the book suggests you do these things, or just read the words and think about them, but write or draw some other time.

You can put this book aside when you've had enough, and pick it up again when you are ready.

While this book can't make whatever happened un-happen, it can answer some of your questions, and help you figure out how to get back to feeling okay.

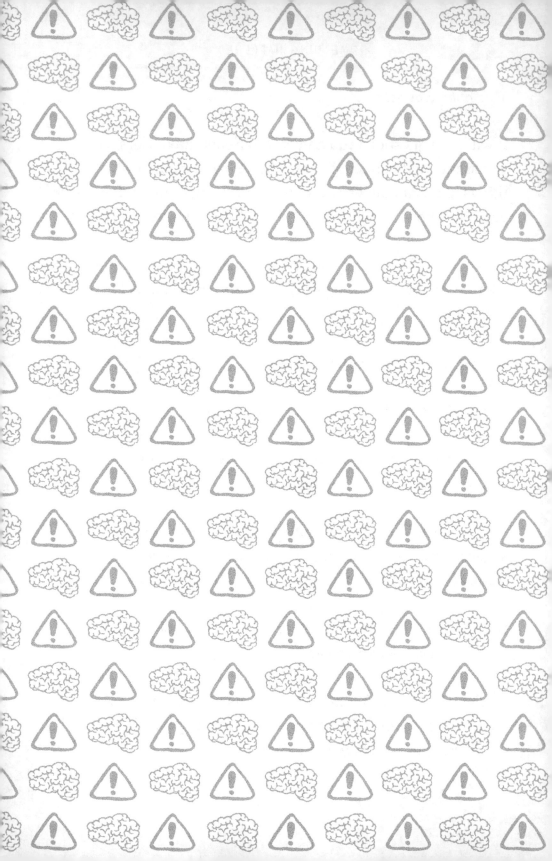

CHAPTER 2

# Brains in High Alert

Before we talk specifically about what happened, there's something important you need to know:

Big bad things, like the thing that recently happened, are rare.

That's good.

But it also means we don't get much practice dealing with them. That's why, when something like this happens, everyone talks about it so much.

Big bad things hit people hard.

Even when the bad thing didn't happen to us directly, it can still hit us hard.

That's confusing, isn't it?

Why would something that didn't happen to us still affect us?

Why would we feel sad about something that happened to people we don't even know, or scared about something that happened halfway around the world?

There are several answers as to why we feel sad and scared about things that didn't happen to us.

The first is that we are capable of putting ourselves into other people's shoes, imagining how they must feel. We feel sympathy, empathy, and compassion for people who have experienced big bad things.

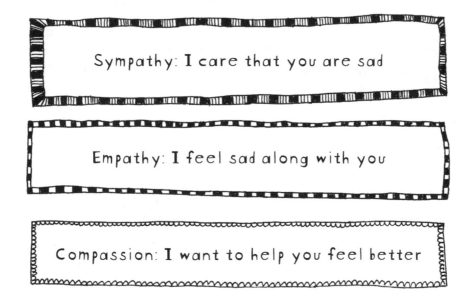

Sympathy: I care that you are sad

Empathy: I feel sad along with you

Compassion: I want to help you feel better

Sympathy, empathy, and compassion make us pay attention to problems that other people are having, even when those problems don't affect us directly.

And there's another reason we pay attention to bad things.

We wonder if the bad thing could happen again. Closer to home. To us.

That's scary.

So, when we hear about something bad that happened—even if it happened in a very different part of the world—our brains go into High Alert.

Our hearts speed up. Our pupils—the parts of our eyes that take in light—get bigger. Our hearing gets sharper. Every part of our body does what it needs to do to make us *ready*, in case the bad thing comes our way.

When our brains are in this High Alert state, we feel on edge. Nervous. Worried. Scared. It feels as if the danger is about to happen. Right here. Right now.

Brains in High Alert focus on the possibility of danger, making us feel unsafe.

But here's the thing: sometimes our brains go into High Alert by mistake. Sometimes we think we are in danger—or about to be in danger—when really, we are quite safe.

We are reacting to something far away, that didn't happen to us and probably won't happen to us. Or something that happened in the past, but now it's over.

Being in High Alert when really you are safe is a common mistake.

When it happens, you need to calm down your brain, so you can get back to thinking clearly and feeling better.

There, there, it's okay.

You need to show your brain—in very specific ways—that the High Alert isn't necessary.

That right here, right now, you are safe.

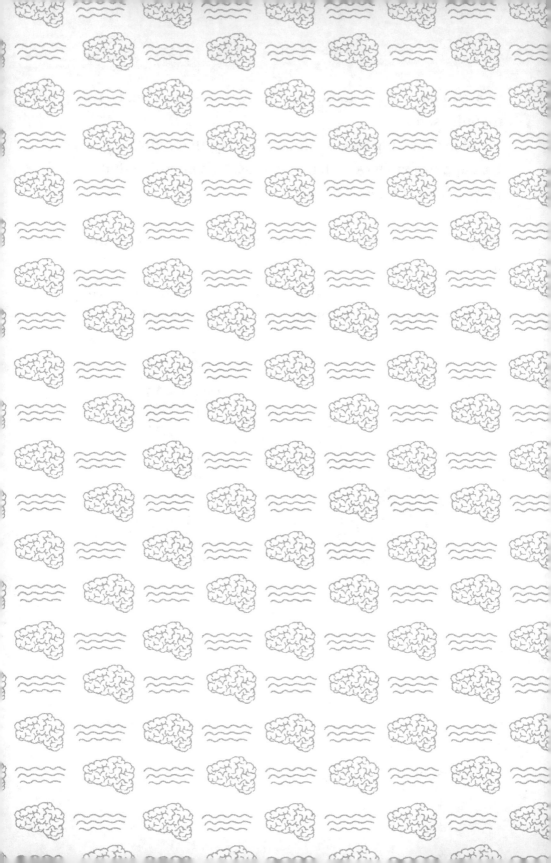

# CHAPTER 3

# Calming Your Brain

Brain High Alerts are useful when danger is real, and close by.

They aren't useful when danger is unlikely, or far away.

If you are reading this book and you start to feel scared, know that your brain has accidentally shifted into High Alert.

It's a false alarm.

Right here, right now, as you sit wherever you are sitting, reading this book, you are safe.

When your brain mistakenly shifts into High Alert, there are things you can do to calm down your brain.

These two activities—Safe and Connected—will quiet your brain and help you see that you are okay.

If you like, you can practice them now so you know how they go:

# SAFE

1. Breathe in through your nose and out through your nose.

2. Notice the cool air as it comes in through your nostrils, and the warm air as it moves out.

3. Feel your bottom pressing into the chair (or the floor), and your feet resting on the ground. Think about the chair, or the floor, holding you.

4. Listen for the small sounds around you. A fan whirring. A dryer clunking. A car whizzing by.

5. Move slowly from sound to sound. Silently say the name of the thing as you hear it. Fan. Dog. Airplane. Car.

6. Can you count six different sounds?

26

7. Keep breathing, in and out. In ... and out.

8. Notice the cool air moving in, and the warm air moving out.

9. Notice that right here, right now—in this chair, in this room, with these sounds around you—you are safe.

# CONNECTED

1. Breathe in through your nose and out through your nose.

2. Imagine there is a string at the top of your head, gently pulling your head, and neck, and whole body upwards. Think of someone or something that lives above you (or to the north). Maybe your upstairs neighbors, or a bird, or the people in an airplane traveling through the sky. Smile as you think of those people, or that bird, and think the words, "I hope you are happy."

3. Imagine the string pulling you gently to your right. Think of someone or something that lives to the right (or the east) of you. It might be your neighbor, or your cousin, or someone you don't know in a place far to the east. Smile as you think of that person, and think, "I hope you are happy."

4. Imagine the string pulling you gently to your left. Think of someone or something that lives to the left (or west) of you. It might be your grandparent, or a friend who has moved, or someone you don't know. Smile as you think of that person and think, "I hope you are happy."

5. Let the string pull you down towards the ground. Think of someone or something that lives below (or south) of you. It might be a rabbit, or an earthworm, or someone far to the south, someone you know, or you don't know

at all. Smile as you think of that person or animal, and think, "I hope you are happy."

6. Imagine the string pulling you gently in all directions. Let your body expand as you breathe.

7. You are part of a big world where many, many people are wishing each other well.

It's normal to feel scared when you hear about something bad. We all feel that way.

But being afraid is not the same as being in danger. You are not in danger.

Pause, and take care of yourself. Help your brain notice that you are okay.

And when you are ready, read on.

# CHAPTER 4

# Gathering Information

Another way to quiet false alarms is to get accurate information about the bad thing that happened. What happened, and where? Why did it happen, and who is working to keep you safe?

Let's talk about those things.

Do you know what happened?

If you have any idea at all, draw or write about it here.

If you have no idea, ask the person who gave you this book to tell you what happened—just the basics—then draw or write about it.

**What happened?**

Why did that bad thing happen?

_____

_____

_____

_____

_____

_____

_____

NewsForKids.com

DOGOnews.com

TeachingKidsNews.com

Newsela.com

Youngzine.org

Sometimes the reasons are clear. Other times, they're complicated.

Ask the grown-up who gave you this book why they think the bad thing happened.

If you and the grown-up you are with don't know why, work together to find out.

Be careful about where you look for information, though.

After something bad happens, many people start talking in very public ways. They give their opinions, which may or may not be based on facts.

People sometimes say things that aren't true or give details you don't need to hear. Even the news programs that the grownups around you trust sometimes say things in needlessly scary ways and show dramatic pictures that aren't meant for kids.

Scary words and dramatic pictures have a way of getting stuck in our brains.

Unless you are reading a news source specifically geared toward children, it is better to get information from the adults who care about you, rather than from the computer, radio, or TV.

After you talk to a grown-up you trust, try to put what you have learned into your own words.

Why did this particular bad thing happen?

Was it caused by nature, or by humans, or both?

Nature

Humans

Both

Did someone do something on purpose, or was it an accident?

On purpose

Accident

Whether the answers are simple or complicated, understanding why a bad thing happened helps us make sense of it. It puts us one step closer to knowing if the feeling of High Alert is accurate, or if it is a false alarm.

# CHAPTER 5

# Location, Location, Location

Another piece of information that helps us know if we are in danger is the location of the bad thing, so let's talk about that.

Where did the bad thing happen? Say the name of the place
or ask a grown-up to tell you.

Let's figure out where that is in relation you.

Find your home on this map. You aren't going to be able to locate your street or even your town exactly, but do your best to find where you live. If you aren't sure, ask a grown-up to help you. Put a dot near your home.

Next, think of someplace about an hour away. Maybe it's your grandparents' house, or the beach you go to every summer. Put a dot on the place that is an hour away.

Look at the space between the two dots. They are probably almost on top of each other. That's because the world is so big.

Think about what it feels like to cross that distance, from your home to the place that's an hour away.

Then, think of a place you've been that is much further away—a long car trip, or train ride, or somewhere you went by plane.

Put a dot on that place.

Think about how long it took you to get there.

Now think about the place where the bad thing happened. Find it on the map. Is it close-by, or far away? How do you know?

If the bad thing that happened was far away, remembering that can help you feel safer. You can remind yourself, "That was far away."

And if the bad thing was close-by, you can think about all the protections that were quickly put in place to keep nearby people safe, because that is exactly what happens.

When something bad happens, good people from all around the world quickly join together to help the people who were directly affected by what happened, and to help those who are nearby stay safe.

So, whether you live nearby or far away, many, many people arc working to keep you safe.

That was far away

# CHAPTER 6

# Identifying Helpers

Your parents, grandparents, teachers, and neighbors care about your safety, and work hard to protect you.

In addition to these people who know you well, there are thousands of grown-ups who don't know you at all working hard to keep you—and all the plants and animals and people in our world—safe.

There are:

doctors, nurses, police officers, principals, teachers, government officials, guards, airline security workers, environmental scientists, marine biologists, structural engineers, veterinarians, military personnel, fire fighters, restaurant inspectors

These people, and others like them, work night and day to keep problems from happening. And when something does go wrong, these problem-solvers work hard to understand why, and to put extra protections in place to keep it from happening again.

There are other kinds of helpers, too. People from all over who show up when something bad happens to help the people who were directly affected.

These people volunteer their time when something bad happens, or send supplies and money to help.

Think about the specific bad thing that happened.

Who is helping the people who were directly affected?

What are they doing to help?

Who is working to reduce the chances of the bad thing happening again? What steps are they taking?

Problem-solvers and helpers live all over the world.

Smart people with big hearts live on your street. They live in your town, in your country and in other countries, too.

Look again at the map where you drew the dots. Lightly shade the parts of the world where problem-solvers and helpers live. (Hint: it's everywhere!)

All these people caring about one another, and helping each other, and watching out for safety is one of the reasons why— even though a bad thing happened—you are still quite safe.

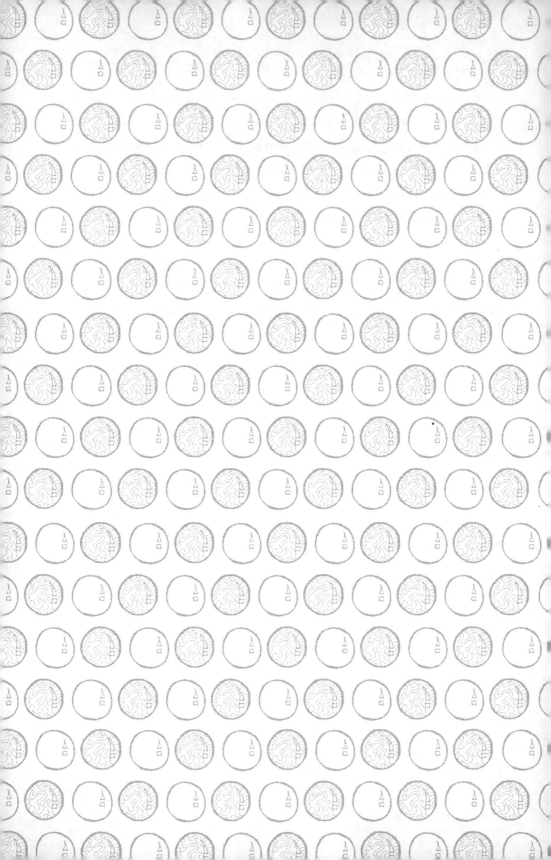

CHAPTER 7

# Understanding Likelihood

Big bad things are rare, but clearly, they do *sometimes* happen.

That's scary. It might make you wonder:

Sometimes we make the mistake of thinking that if a bad thing *can* happen to *someone*, it WILL happen to US.

But remember we talked about the importance of accurate information?

Thinking that if a bad thing can happen to someone, it will happen to us isn't accurate.

Just because something *can* happen, that doesn't mean it *will* happen.

**Possible** is not the same as **likely**.

Let's talk a bit more about likely and unlikely so you can understand what it means when your parents say that you are safe, that the big bad thing is extremely unlikely to happen to you.

Here's what likely and unlikely mean.

Imagine two marbles: one swirly and one plain.

Imagine putting them both in a jar.

Imagine closing your eyes and reaching into the jar. How likely are you to pull out the swirly marble?

Pretty likely, right? After all, there are only two marbles.

How likely are you to pull out the plain marble?

That's pretty likely, too.

Since there are only two marbles, you are just as likely to pull out the swirly marble as the plain one.

Now imagine having one hundred marbles: 99 plain and one swirly.

Again, you put them in a jar, close your eyes and reach in. How likely is it that you'll get the swirly marble now?

A lot less likely, right?

You are 99 times more likely to get a plain marble than the swirly one. Reaching in with your eyes closed and ending up with the swirly marble is unlikely. The chances are really small.

But swirly marbles and plain marbles don't matter very much, do they? So, let's switch to something that does matter: staying safe at an amusement park.

Imagine this: you get invited to an amusement park. You want to go, but you know that every once in a while, someone gets hurt on a ride.

Should you take the chance? Should you go?

Well, it depends on how often accidents happen. How likely are you to get hurt?

Pretend plain marbles mean you are going to be safe, and the swirly marble means you are going to get hurt.

If there were just two marbles—one plain and one swirly—that would mean that if you go to the park, you are just as likely to get hurt as not. That isn't safe. No one would want to go to that park.

What if there were 99 plain marbles and only 1 swirly one?

That sounds better, although really it means that for every hundred people at the park, one will get hurt.

That's still not very good.

Most people wouldn't go to a park if one out of every hundred people got hurt.

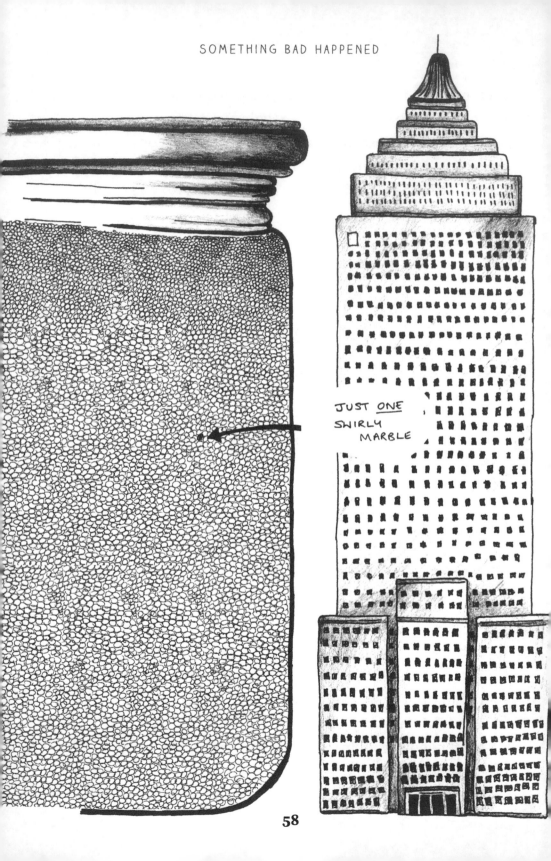

JUST ONE
SWIRLY
MARBLE

In truth, the chance of getting hurt on a ride at an amusement park is closer to several million to one. Several million plain marbles (meaning you'd be safe) and just one swirly marble.

Would you go to an amusement park knowing there was such a tiny chance of getting hurt, and a HUGE chance of being fine? Most people would.

And if you don't like amusement parks, imagine some other activity that carries a tiny bit of risk. Going boating, or on a train. Riding a bicycle. Doing gymnastics.

We do things every day that are just a little bit risky. Getting hurt is possible, but super unlikely. And then we add in safety features—like wearing a helmet or strapping ourselves into a ride—which make getting hurt even more unlikely.

We don't need to be 100 percent sure to feel safe. We just need the chance of getting hurt to be really, really small.

So now we come back to the bad thing that happened.

Even if it wasn't the first time this sort of thing happened, and even if quite a few people were affected, whatever happened still has only a teeny tiny chance of happening to you or someone you love.

Bad things like whatever happened are rare. There are lots of protections in place. And there are billions of people in the world. Billions.

2018 population:
7.6 billion

Each of us is one tiny marble in a world chock-full of other marbles.

That means that the chance of this particular bad thing happening to you or someone you love is so very small. It is so, so, so unlikely.

Remember this picture when you feel afraid.

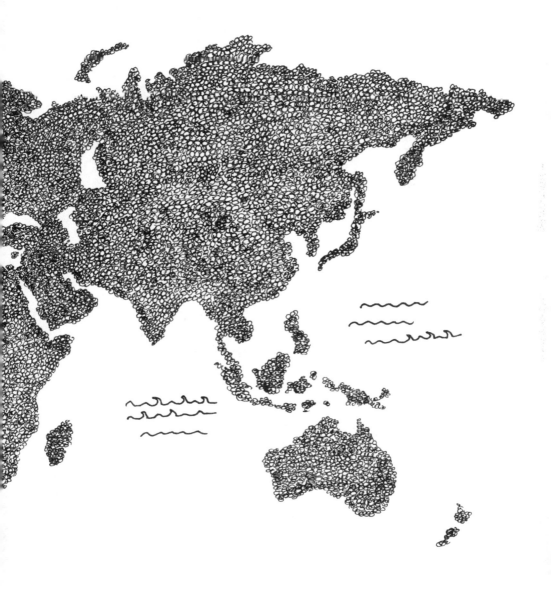

CHAPTER 8

# Dealing with Feelings

Lots of feelings get stirred up when we hear about something big and bad that happened. We've been talking about fear, but there are other feelings, too.
Look at these faces.

Circle the faces that show how you feel when you think about the bad thing that happened. As you circle the face, say the name of the feeling out loud.

Maybe you don't have any feelings about what happened, or at least not any feelings that you are aware of. That's okay, too. There are no right or wrong ways to feel.

Put a square around the faces that show how the grown-ups around you seem to be feeling.

You may (or may not) have feelings in common. Either way is okay.

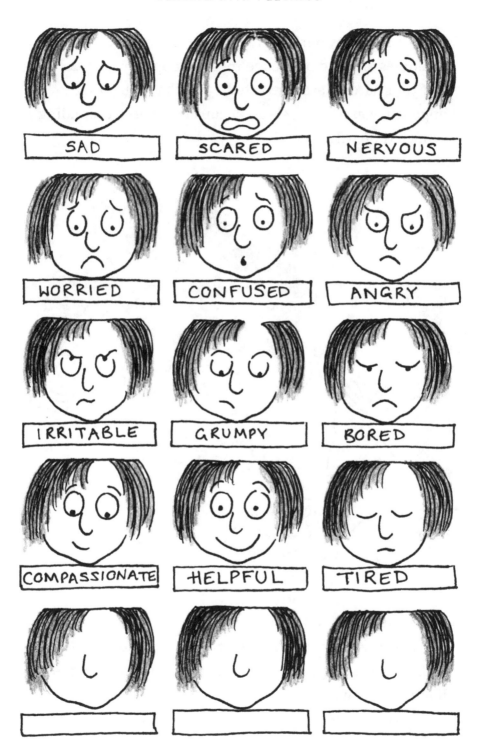

We are affected by our own feelings, and we notice and are sometimes affected by the feelings of people around us.

If your parents are distracted by the bad thing that happened, you might feel sad because they aren't spending as much time with you.

If your parents are on edge, you might feel nervous, too.

If they are irritable, you might feel confused or sad.

All these feelings are common after a big bad thing. And all are temporary.

The grown-ups around you will do what they need to do

to gather information, and to make sure everyone is safe. They will do what they need to do to cope with their feelings, and eventually things will return to normal.

Whatever is happening will someday be in the past, and life will settle down.

In the meantime, talk to the grown-ups around you about what you are feeling.

Ask questions, if you want, about what they are feeling.

Talking about feelings helps.

When we name a feeling, we make it less powerful.

When we name a feeling, we can also begin to figure out how to deal with it.

If you know, for example, that you are scared, you can do the Safe and Connected activities on page XX to help your brain settle down.

You can look at the map on page XX to remind yourself where the bad thing was, and look at the drawing on page XX to see how unlikely it is to happen to you.

You can think about all the people who are helping, and the things you and your family are doing to stay safe.

If you are confused, you can ask your parents questions, and use the advice on page XX to gather information together.

If you are sad, you can ask for a hug. Being with people we love, and people who love us, always helps.

CHAPTER 9

# Self-Care

Sometimes, when a bad thing happens, we forget to take care of ourselves.

No matter what happens, it's important to keep doing the things that keep us healthy and strong, and that make us who we are.

We need to keep eating healthy foods. We need to go outside every day, and get enough exercise, and get plenty of sleep. These healthy habits help our brains deal with stress and move us towards happier feelings.

We also get back to feeling okay when we spend time every day doing things that matter to us—not just things that are fun, but also things that matter.

How do you know what matters?

Think about how you would complete the following sentences. Look at the ideas first, then write words that are true about you.

**1.** I am a person who is...

---

(kind, compassionate, fair, funny, nice, friendly)

**2.** I care about...

---

(soccer, my sister, horses, doing well in school)

**3.** I feel good about myself when I am...

---

(building things, helping my brother, solving problems, having fun with my friends)

When you are feeling sad, or angry, or confused, or scared, after you have named your feelings and talked about them, do something from one of your lists.

Really.

Even if you don't feel like riding your bike, making an origami giraffe, or getting out your soccer ball, even if you don't feel like helping your dad or calling a friend, do it anyway.

Once you get involved in any activity that goes along with something that matters to you, your brain will shift gears and you'll start to feel better.

CHAPTER 10

# Healing the World

There's one final thing to think about. In some ways, it's the most important thing of all.

When something big and bad happens, no matter where you are, no matter what you are thinking and feeling, you are not alone.

There are people in your house, your town, and all around the world finding out about what happened.

People who know and are now bystanders, just like you.

Have you heard that word? Bystander.

Bystanders are people who aren't directly involved in something that happens, but they see it, or hear about it afterwards, like you did.

You are a bystander to the bad thing that happened.

That may sound scary, but remember this:

Bystanders can be powerful.

They can't make bad things un-happen, but they can help the people who were affected, and they can speak up to show that they care.

Some bystanders decide not to get involved.

They get busy with other things, trying to forget about whatever happened, keeping their feelings locked inside.

These bystanders do nothing, hoping the situation will somehow change on its own.

It doesn't work that way.

It's bystanders who decide to *do something* that make bad situations better.

And bystanders who decide to *do something* feel better faster, too.

Doing something positive—no matter what that positive thing is—helps.

Doing something positive shifts your attention away from the sad and scary parts of whatever happened, and towards the good thing you are doing.

It makes you feel stronger. More hopeful. More connected to other people doing positive things.

Doing something positive makes you a part of all the good that exists in the world.

Even small positive things make a difference.

Stepping forward.
Being kind.
Showing support for people who are hurting, or people working hard to solve problems.
Caring for the earth. Accepting people who are different from you.
Doing something positive always helps.

You and your family might:

- raise money for whoever was affected by the thing that just happened
- draw a picture or send a card to show that you care
- go to a rally or march to show your support
- donate to the organizations that are helping
- do something to take care of the environment.

**What can you and your family do to help?**

When something bad happens, it's important to:

- calm your brain
- gather accurate information
- identify helpers
- deal with feelings
- do something positive.

Your words, your efforts, your actions matter.
    You can help to heal the world.